D1647788

# THE MURAL OF FRUIT

Raúl Dorantes

Illustrated by Lydia Halverson

Rigby

© 1997 by Rigby,
a division of Reed Elsevier, Inc.
500 Coventry Lane
Crystal Lake, IL 60014

00 99 98 97 96
10 9 8 7 6 5 4 3 2 1

Printed in the United States of America

ISBN 0-7635-3165-0

Chano and Jaime sat on a bench eating their lunches on the school playground. They were both wondering what they wanted to make for the next school art fair. Before lunch, Ms. Radinski had told them that the fair would be called "Sharing Our Cultures."

Chano watched his classmates play on the swings and go down the slide. Then Chano noticed that Jaime was eating a fruit he had never seen before.

Chano looked at the small fruit, with its green peel and pink inside. "What's that you're eating?" Chano asked Jaime.

"It's a guava," answered Jaime as he lifted one in his hand. "Everybody eats them in the Dominican Republic, where I come from."

"It looks like a lime, doesn't it?" asked Chano.

"No! The peel is smooth, and you can eat it. The inside is pink, soft, and sweet," Jaime said. He took a bite into its soft flesh as Chano watched.

Chano took out a plastic bag with slices of some sort of melon inside. Jaime looked at the yellow skin and the white center as Chano bit into the flesh of the fruit. "What's that *you're* eating?" Jaime asked. "I've never seen it before."

"It's called *cham-eh*. My parents ate it when they were children in Korea. We can buy cham-eh here in Chicago at a store on Kimball Avenue. Do you want a taste?"

Jaime took a slice of cham-eh and bit into it. "Oh, it's delicious! It's cool and sweet," said Jaime. He offered Chano one of the guavas from his bag. "Now you try one."

"Mmm… it looks like a lime but doesn't taste like one—it's sweet!" Chano announced after tasting the guava.

"In our house," Jaime told Chano, "we eat Dominican food, just like we did when we lived in Santo Domingo. My mom says that Dominican food has some African roots, like us."

Chano nodded, saying, "At home, we like to do things the way my parents did them in Korea. We celebrate Korean Thanksgiving, which is called *Chu-suk*, and like to eat traditional Korean dishes."

As they continued to talk, the two friends began to realize that some of the other children must be eating fruit that neither of them had heard of. Chano suggested that they could learn about these fruits if everyone brought a fruit for show-and-tell.

"Let's ask Ms. Radinski if we can have a show-and-tell with fruit in our classroom!" he said enthusiastically.

"Yes! You could talk about cham-eh, and I could tell about guavas. The other kids could bring fruits they want to talk about," said Jaime.

"That would be really fun!" exclaimed Chano.

Chano and Jaime ran inside to tell Ms. Radinski about their idea. Chano suggested that all the students bring their families' favorite fruits. Ms. Radinski loved the idea. When the class came in from lunch, she asked them, "Who likes fruit?"

One by one, the children began to talk about their favorites. Strawberries, cherries, grapes, and oranges were a few of the many fruits named.

"The fruits we eat can show something special about our background," said Ms. Radinski. "Many Americans eat cranberry sauce for Thanksgiving, but did you know that I love to eat blueberry *pierogis* for dinner in the summertime? My grandmother came from Poland. She taught me how to make this dumpling, and now I make them for my family."

Ms. Radinski encouraged the children to think about the fruit they ate at their houses. She told everyone that the class would hold a fruit bazaar next Monday. Each child would bring a fruit or a fruit dish that represented his or her family's background. Then they would share the food in a fruit feast!

Ray, who sat in the front row, asked anxiously, "Ms. Radinski, will you bring in a blueberry pierogi? They sound good."

Ms. Radinski laughed and replied, "I'll bring in enough for everybody to have a taste."

Monday was a delicious day!  Every student brought fruit.  Some brought fresh fruit, others brought fruit salads, and still others brought desserts and breads made with fruits.  The classroom smelled like an orchard and had the freshness of the countryside.

"Who wants to tell us about his or her fruit?" asked Ms. Radinski.

Ray, who had thought about blueberry pierogis all weekend, was the first to raise his hand. "I asked my Aunt Janita about a fruit that might tell something about my family. She said that bananas are a good fruit to represent our family's background because they grow both in Africa and in America. She also told me that the banana is popular because you can eat it so many different ways. When it's green, you fry it in oil. When it's yellow and ripe, you just peel it and eat it. When it starts to turn black, it's too ripe and you bake with it. My Aunt Janita made this bread. I guess our bananas were too ripe!"

Ms. Radinski told Ray to put his bread next to the pierogis on a central table. She explained that when everyone is finished presenting, they would be able to eat their show-and-tell offerings together.

Next Patricia held up a reddish oval about the size of a large orange. "This is a mango. In Nicaragua, we eat mango snow cones, and we also drink it in juice." She then put a large bowl of cut and peeled mango slices on the table. The fruit's inside was yellowish-orange and ragged where the pit had been removed.

Yen was next. "I want to talk about the mandarin orange," she said, holding a small bright orange in the palm of her hand. "My dad told me that it's originally from Asia and that its name comes from the Mandarin people. They ruled China many years ago." She placed a bag of these oranges on the table alongside the bowl of mangoes.

Children continued to introduce their fruits, one at a time, and to place them on the table. It was starting to look like a feast of fruit! Evelyn was the last to make a presentation.

"I brought apples for everybody," said Evelyn, moving to the front. "My mother's family came from Germany. Apples are a favorite fruit there. Yesterday I helped her bake an apple pastry called *strudel*. First we made a thin dough. Then we put in nuts, raisins, and pieces of apple. Finally we rolled it up. I've had it before, and it's really delicious!" She carefully placed the long pastry on the table.

Everyone looked expectantly at Ms. Radinski. "Well, children," she said, beaming, "it looks like we've got ourselves a feast of fruit!" They all took a plate and a napkin and began helping themselves to the fruits and fruit dishes. As they began to sample the foods, looks of surprise and pleasure—and, yes, even the occasional grimace—crossed their faces.

Jaime looked at Chano and smiled. He could see that everyone was having a good time and was glad that their idea had been a success.

When the fruit feast had ended and the class had cleaned up the mess, Ms. Radinski said, "We've learned that Chicago is a place of many cultures—and many flavors. In stores all over this city, you can find a wonderful variety of foods. Ask your parents to take you out to explore your neighborhood or other nearby neighborhoods in search of new and interesting foods. Then you can tell the class all about what you've seen, and we'll all learn more about our city."

Suddenly Jaime had an idea. "Ms. Radinski, may I paint a picture of my guava for the art fair?"

"What a wonderful idea," she said, nodding.

14

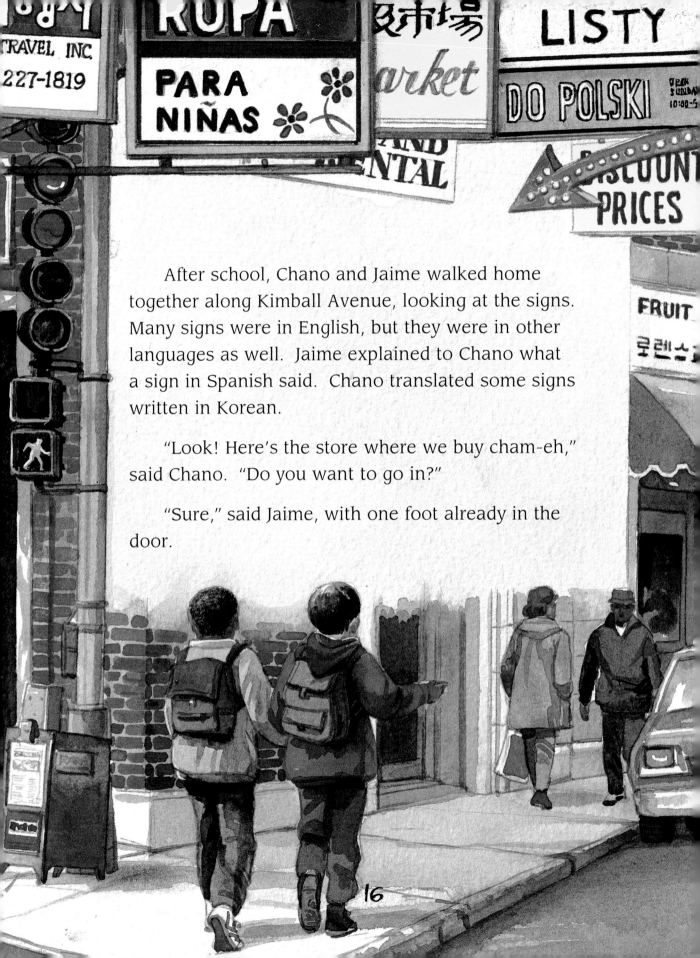

After school, Chano and Jaime walked home together along Kimball Avenue, looking at the signs. Many signs were in English, but they were in other languages as well. Jaime explained to Chano what a sign in Spanish said. Chano translated some signs written in Korean.

"Look! Here's the store where we buy cham-eh," said Chano. "Do you want to go in?"

"Sure," said Jaime, with one foot already in the door.

For Jaime, it was a new and exciting experience. Everywhere Jaime turned, he saw foods that he'd never seen before. He picked up a bag of noodles labeled in Korean, but put it down when Chano pointed out some jars of *kim chi*. Jaime looked cautiously at the cabbage floating in reddish liquid. Chano laughed and said that it was spicy pickled cabbage and that his family ate it all the time. Finally they found the mountains of cham-eh.

"This store is so close to my house," said Jaime. "I can't believe I've never come in here. I'm going to ask my dad to buy cham-eh sometime."

Looking at the piles of cham-eh, Chano picked one up and said, "Listen, you're painting guavas for the art fair. Maybe I should paint some cham-eh."

"That would be perfect!" said Jaime, beaming.

Chano and Jaime left the store and continued walking. On one of the buildings was a large mural painted in bright colors. Jaime stopped in his tracks and stared at the mural.

"What's up?" asked Chano.

"Listen, Chano. What do you think about the whole class painting something really big like this? Something we all paint together? Each of us could paint our fruit. You'd paint cham-eh. I'd paint guavas. Patricia could paint mangoes."

"This project just keeps getting better and better!" said Chano.

The two friends continued talking about the mural until they reached Chano's house.

"We'll have the coolest classroom in the school. The walls will be covered with fruit," shouted Chano as he climbed the front steps.

"You mean *paintings* of fruit," laughed Jaime, as he waved good-bye to his friend.

When Jaime and Chano arrived at school the next day, Ms. Radinski was preparing a poster for the school fair. She had painted "Sharing Our Cultures" across the top. When class started, she asked if students knew what they wanted to make for the fair.

"Remember, it's a fair for the whole school," said Ms. Radinski. "Whatever you do should be your best."

Sharing
Our
Cultures

Jaime raised his hand. When Ms. Radinski called on him, he said, "Why don't we make one big painting with all our fruit?"

"The whole class could work together," added Chano. "Each one of us could do part of it by painting a different fruit."

"It would be colorful and beautiful, and it would go along with the theme of the fair—Sharing Our Cultures!" said Jaime.

"It sounds to me like you boys are talking about a mural. What a great idea!" said Ms. Radinski. She turned to the class, "Do you like that idea?"

"Yes!" said everyone.

Sharing
Our
Cultures

The Mural
of Fruit

That very day, the class began to prepare for the mural. Some students practiced drawing their fruit in their notebooks, while others looked for pictures that they could copy from.

Ms. Radinski finished the poster for the project by adding "The Mural of Fruit." Then she hung large pieces of paper on the wall for the mural.

During the next few days, family and friends who wanted to help with the mural project came to the classroom. Evelyn's mother, who was an artist, taught the children how to mix paints to create interesting colors. Ray and his uncle cut bananas out of colored paper to add to the mural.

The group decided to add images of famous Chicago landmarks to the mural to show that this colorful array of fruit—and culture—was part of their city. Together, they decided on the Water Tower, the Sears Tower, and the Picasso sculpture.

When the mural was finished, bright colors of paint, chalk, colored paper, and yarn blended together to create magnificent pieces of fruit, all toppling over one another as if ready for a bountiful feast. There were mangoes, blueberries, bananas, and a host of other fruits, including, of course, cham-eh and guavas. The style of each fruit was as different as the child who had created it. Tall and imposing in the background sat the Chicago landmarks.

On the day of the "Sharing Our Cultures" fair, the sounds of music and the smells of foods from all over the world filled the school hallways.  In Ms. Radinski's classroom, all the visitors praised the "Mural of Fruit" for its creativity and beauty.  The parents were delighted to recognize the fruits they were already familiar with and to discover new ones.  The students felt their pride in their cultural backgrounds—and their appetites!—swell as they presented their mural with pleasure.